This Book Belongs to

_____

The Sled Book

NOTES CONCERNING WINTER'S

FAVORITE PASTIME

By Brice J. Hoskin

SKIPSTONE

Published by Skipstone, an imprint of The Mountaineers Books

Printed in United States of America

First printing 2007

10 09 08 07   5 4 3 2 1

Copy Editor: Judith Dern

Book Design: Daberko Design

Illustrator: Traci Daberko

ISBN 10: 1-59485-069-0

ISBN 13: 978-1-59485-069-1

Excerpt on page 31: Charles Wendell Townsend, (ed.), *Captain Cartwright and His Labrador Journal*, Sixth Voyage, 1786. (Boston: Dana Estes & Company, 1911), pp. 357-358.

Kick sledding primer text on page 38-39 adapted with permission from the *Silverton Standard*'s 2005 Winter Guide Article on page 44 from E.H. Garrett, "Coasting on Boston Common," *Harper's Weekly*, (Feb. 13, 1875): 132.

Library of Congress Cataloging-in-Publication Data

Hoskin, Brice J., 1967-

  The sled book : notes concerning winter's favorite pastime / by Brice J. Hoskin.

    p. cm.

  ISBN-13: 978-1-59485-069-1

  ISBN-10: 1-59485-069-0

 1. Sledding. 2. Sleds—History. I. Title.

GV856.H67 2007

796.9'5—dc22

                    2007018668

Skipstone books may be purchased for corporate, educational, or other promotional sales. For special discounts and information, contact our Sales Department at 1-800-553-4453 or mbooks@mountaineersbooks.org.

1001 SW Klickitat Way, Suite 201

Seattle, Washington 98134

Phone: 206.223.6303

www.skipstonepress.org

www.mountaineersbooks.org

LIVE LIFE. MAKE RIPPLES.

♻ Printed on recycled paper

For my wife and sledding
partner, Karen

✳

Contents

The Joy of
Sledding

*I*magine a New Year's Eve in the high mountain town of Silverton, Colorado, the night quiet under a sky of pinpoint stars. It's a crisp ten-below night in a town so sleepy it seems abandoned. My friend Dan and I walk our sleds up Tenth Street, a winter-white avenue plowed and packed into hard snow. The gradual hill turns steeper the higher we climb, until we are several hundred feet above the silent town. We each have a sled with metal runners, perfect for this kind of firm snow, this kind of frozen night.

Tenth Street intersects several other streets, but the most exciting intersection by far is where it meets Silverton's central thoroughfare—Greene Street. Four blocks down from the top of the hill, sledders have to contend with Greene, paved and plowed, a single ribbon of black asphalt running through a snow-white town. Dan and I had done this before and knew the secret: go as fast as possible.

Having reached the top of the hill, we lay down our sleds, take a flying leap and jump on. Side by side, we accelerate down Tenth Street with no possibility of turning away or stopping. As we hit the asphalt at top speed, the night gets suddenly brighter. Sparks shower from the metal runners, surrounding us in a warm orange glow. We have just enough momentum to screech across the asphalt of Greene Street onto snow on the other side of Tenth, gliding for another block before we slow to a gradual stop. We are both in our thirties, supposedly far too old for this kind of fun, but the still night rings with our shouts, "Again!!"

Speed. That's really what sledding is about—barreling downhill, face to the wind and thinking only *faster, faster*. I like to lie belly down on the sled, head first, because I can feel the snow sliding away underneath me and gravity pulling me faster, ever faster down the white hill.

This book celebrates the unabashed joy of sledding. It reviews highlights from the history of sledding, and is also a practical guide to finding a great sled and a perfect sledding hill. Not least, you'll also find tips about how to stay safe and warm while sledding. It's also a story about building a successful sledmaking business, and how beautiful, well-made sleds still have a place in this world.

HEBREW מזחלת • DANISH slæde • DUTCH slee • FINNISH kelkka • FRENCH lug

ARABIC مِزْلَجَةٌ

How to Spell "Sled"

JAPANESE 雪橇 雪車 橇

KOREAN 썰매 썰매를 탄다

CHINESE 雪橇

GERMAN *schlitten* • GREEK έλκηθρο • ITALIAN *slitta* • NORWEGIAN *kjelke* • PORTUGUESE *trenó* • RUSSIAN салазки • SPANISH *trineo* • SWEDISH *släde*

Around the World

The History of Sleds

Sleds Through the Ages

rom 19th century kicksleds to the Winter Olympics luge competitions, the history of sleds is about innovation. Sleds were first invented as a practical vehicle to make it easier to pull loads and people across snowy terrain. Inventors in the last two centuries have made sleds diverse enough for every kind of snow and snowy hill.

Toboggans

The longest pedigree among sleds belongs to the toboggan, a word derived from either the Algonquin word *odabaggan* or the Anishinabe word *nobugidaban*. Toboggans were widely used by the native peoples of North America, who either pulled them or used them as dog sleds to make hauling heavy loads over snow and ice easier. The Inuit built their toboggans of whalebone, but other tribes traditionally used birch or tamarack.

Captain George Cartwright, an early explorer in the Canadian taiga, described an Innu toboggan in 1786: "Their sleds are made of two thin boards of birch; each about six inches broad, a quarter of an inch thick, and six feet long: these are fastened parallel to each other by slight battens, sewed on with thongs of deer-skin; and the foremost end is curved up to rise over the inequalities of the snow." The Innu used the toboggans to carry children, bundled in deer-skins, and all their gear. All those walking would wear snowshoes, with the men traveling in front, followed by the women and older children.

The design of the toboggan has changed very little since that time. Most toboggans are now made with seven boards of ash or maple, each about two inches wide. Using good steaming equipment and well-built forms, modern toboggan manufacturers can make the curl at the front as tight as they like.

Tobogganing as a sport began on the slopes of Mount Royal in Montreal, Canada, in the late 1800s, and spread to cities across the globe. The Russians were particularly avid "coasters," and built the first toboggan slide in St. Petersburg. The high wooden structure let you pull your toboggan up the side of an ice-covered chute and then fly down. (Note: the chute didn't have another side—you walked up right next to the toboggan run.) In 1884, Cresta, the most famous toboggan slide—later to become a bobsled run—was built in St. Moritz, Switzerland. Not to be left behind, city fathers and fashionable private clubs in the United States built slides in Saratoga, Utica, Albany, Orange, Boston, New York City, Chicago, and many other cities. One of the largest was the slide at Drexel Boulevard and 44th Street in Chicago. It had four parallel runs, each about 1,000 feet long, and provided a warming house with an adjacent skating pond at the bottom.

At that time, going tobogganing was very fashionable and refined. Ladies and gentlemen wore their best clothes and topcoats. It was not uncommon on winter afternoons for entire families to slide down the toboggan chute in high style.

Today's toboggan mecca is Camden, Maine, host to the annual United States National Toboggan Championship, where more than 300 teams compete on toboggans up to 12 feet long. Some recent team names included the Atomic Bald Men, Babes on the Decline, Drunken Monkeys, Sled Astaire, Demolition Doughboy, Frozen Assets, and Three Pains in the Ash. In what has been called "a combination of Rio's Carnival, Mardi Gras, the Winter Olympics and the demolition derby," over one thousand people in two-, three- and four-person teams race down the toboggan run in full costume.

In 2004, *Sports Illustrated* wrote a big story about the event, and *Skiing Magazine* covered the event in 2005. "When we read about the race, there was a warning that your clothes could catch on fire," said Steve Williams, team captain of the Crash Test Dummies. "We were intrigued. We knew we had to try that." On their first trip, Williams' wife's jacket suffered a melted sleeve after prolonged exposure to the chute at 45 miles per hour. "Now, she will wear nothing else during the race. It is her badge of honor," he said.

The Championship is open to anyone, but it has become so popular that a cap has been placed on the number of teams. There are also strict regulations on the size, length and design of toboggans used on the course—but no restrictions on the outrageousness of the clothing worn by competitors.

Toboggans are still used today by outfitters in Maine, Canada, and elsewhere for transport on unique winter adventures. Participants haul sleds made of thin, flexible ash loaded down with gear as they trek through pristine untracked wilderness. The toboggan's long, narrow, flat-bottomed design allows the comfortable hauling of a significant amount of weight, everything from large walled tents and gourmet food to sheet metal woodstoves.

5 SUPERB TOBOGGAN

1

Camden, Maine: Home to the country's most famous toboggan run, the municipal ski area has a 400-foot toboggan slide built for speed. The Camden Outing Club repaired and revived the toboggan chute in 1991, opening it to the public. Contact: Camden Snow Bowl, (207) 236-3438 or visit www.camdensnowbowl.com.

2

Waterford, Michigan: Named The Fridge, this refrigerated toboggan run located northwest of Detroit is one thousand feet long, allowing riders to reach 30 miles per hour. Toboggans are provided. Contact: Oakland County Parks & Recreation, (248) 975-4440 or visit www.oakgov.com/parksrec/ppark/fridge.html.

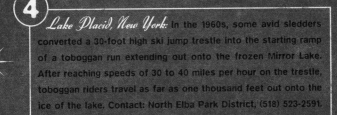

RUNS IN THE UNITED STATES

3 *Angola, Indiana:* The toboggan run in Pokagon State Park in the far northeast corner of the state is a quarter-mile long and by all reports, fast! Sledders can reach speeds of 40 miles per hour. Contact the Park, (260) 833-2012, or visit www.tobogganrun.com.

4 *Lake Placid, New York:* In the 1960s, some avid sledders converted a 30-foot high ski jump trestle into the starting ramp of a toboggan run extending out onto the frozen Mirror Lake. After reaching speeds of 30 to 40 miles per hour on the trestle, toboggan riders travel as far as one thousand feet out onto the ice of the lake. Contact: North Elba Park District, (518) 523-2591.

5 *Eagles Mere, Pennsylvania:* This toboggan run about halfway between Williamsport and Scranton was first constructed in 1903, and also runs out onto a lake. Contact: Eagles Mere Borough, (570) 525-3244.

Kicksleds

Kicksleds were invented in Scandinavia in the late 1800s, and their popularity spread quickly. In Sweden's northern province of Jämtland, timber sleds with elongated runners were used to pull lumber out of the subarctic forests during winter. An unknown inventor put a layer of iron on the bottom of the runners and added a horizontal handlebar, creating the Swedish-style kicksled of the late 19th century. The design was later improved with flexible metal runners, giving the kicksled remarkable agility without compromising its stability.

Sweden's most prominent kicksled enthusiast was Captain Victor Balck, a member of the first modern Olympic Committee, who founded the world's first kicksledding club in 1889 in Stockholm. In 1891, the first Finnish club was established. Its founder, Colonel Edward Furuhielm, arranged races within the military and promoted the use of kicksleds on soldiers' holiday trips from the garrison to their home areas. By 1906, kicksledding was considered one of the three most significant winter sports in Finland after cross-country skiing and skating, and the sport played a major role in the Nordic Games, predecessor to the Winter Olympics.

Kicksled racing stagnated in Scandinavia after 1910, but was reborn in the 1980s. There are now races both on snow-packed roads and frozen lakes. Distances vary from the 200-meter sprint to a 100-kilometer ice race, and speeds average 30 kilometers per hour or 18 miles per hour. The most famous races are the annual Ice Kicksled World Championships in the small town of Multia, Finland, where hundreds of participants of different age groups gather for competitions and recreational events.

A Kicksled Primer

So... How do you make a kicksled go?

To start, stand with one foot on the left or right runner, hold on to the handlebar, and kick or push against the ground with your free foot. For some folks, that may be as far as they want to go toward becoming a kicksledding master. Others, however, will want to get up little more speed by following these instructions.

THE KICK

"Don't lean on the hands or the kicking foot," says the Kicksled Primer, by the Ketkupolkka (Kicksled) Club of Helsinki. The kicksledder's weight should mostly be on the non-kicking foot.

START PHASE

"Imagine that you are an assaulting cheetah," further recommends the Kicksled Primer.

1. Bend forward, keeping your torso horizontal.
2. Lift the kicking foot high in front, but don't swing your leg straight, lift the knee instead (and be careful not to hit your nose with your knee).
3. Your weight will move slightly onto your arms, but not to the point where you're leaning forward.

KICK PHASE

1. Bend your support leg and use its weight to add power to each kick. In a full effort kick, the heel of the support foot detaches from the runner.
2. Your kicking foot should hit the ground with the forefoot, as if you are sprinting.

END PHASE

The primer notes that the "end phase of the kick is especially important."

1. Your kicking ankle should extend completely.
2. As the foot pushes back, the kicksledder should bend mostly at the pelvis and only moderately at the knee. This position will spare the quadriceps of the support leg and will keep the center of gravity level.

PENDULUM PHASE

"As the speed approaches maximum, the free pendulum movement is not enough for bringing the kicking foot to the front," warns the Kicksled Primer.

1. Speed up the leg motion by flexing the hip and thigh muscles. At this point, the kicking motion will begin to feel more like a rotating, rather than a back-and-forth, motion.
2. Always make maximum use of the glide phase.

SWAPPING FEET

The Kicksled Primer recommends swapping feet about once every five kicks. Swap your feet more often during intense kicking periods and less during low effort times.

HOW TO GO UPHILL

- Increase the frequency and shorten your kicks.
- Try to keep your knees straight to avoid any up-down pumping motion.
- Try the "jump swap." This means jump immediately after kicking while bringing the kick foot to the front. Land the kick foot on the runner and bring the support foot down to kick.
- If the hill is too steep, get off and run up!

HOW TO GO DOWNHILL

Put both feet on the runners and flex your knees using them as shock absorbers.

Bobsleds

In 1882, when skiing was still unknown in central Europe, English soldiers built a toboggan track in Davos, Switzerland. The course followed the general construction of tracks elsewhere, which had proved very popular even though the courses were only a straight slide down. At Davos, to make the course more challenging, the builders added curves. The course was first used for toboggan racing, and later for bobsleds.

The bobsled design came about when a steering mechanism was attached to the front of a toboggan (the inventor remains anonymous). The speed and thrills of bobsled racing led to the sport's quick growth throughout Europe, and it soon spread as well to North America and Russia. Early competitors thought it helped to "bob" back and forth on straightaways, hence the name, though they soon realized sleds actually went faster if riders remained low.

The first bobsled club was founded in St. Moritz, Switzerland in 1896, and the sport rapidly spread to winter resorts throughout Europe. By 1914, bobsled races were taking place on a wide variety of natural ice slopes. In 1924, a four-man bobsled race took place at the first Winter Olympics in Chamonix, France. At the 1932 Olympics in Lake Placid, New York, a two-man event was added.

The excitement of bobsled races comes from their high speeds and slippery ice. Most modern tracks are 4,000 to 4,500 feet long, with at least fifteen curves. Top speeds exceed 80 miles per hour, and tight curves subject crews to as much as five times the normal force of gravity.

Today's bobsleds have come far from their simple wood-and-steel beginnings. Sleds now have aerodynamic full-coverage bodies made of strong, light composite materials, and tempered steel runners exactingly designed for high speed.

Two variations of the bobsled also made it to the Olympics: the skeleton and the luge, both of which are raced on bobsled tracks. The skeleton is a one-person sled driven by a rider lying prone, head-first, on the sled. An Englishman introduced this surprising new sled made mostly from metal in 1892, and the sport took its name from the way the sleds were stripped down to a bare frame, like a skeleton. Skeleton racing was an Olympic sport from 1928 through 1960. In the 1964 Winter Olympics, it was replaced by the luge. The luge is a small one or two-person sled, on which the riders lie feet-first and steer by flexing the runners or pulling straps attached to the runners.

Currently, only two bobsled runs in North America are open to the public. Both are at former Winter Olympics sites in Lake Placid, New York, and Park City, Utah. In Lake Placid, you can cruise the bobsled track with a professional driver and brakeman, or go it alone on the luge. How fast? Well, they call it the Luge Rocket and advertise speeds up to 80 miles per hour. In Park City, you can ride the bobsled hurtling along at up to 80 miles per hour. At both tracks, bobsleds shoot through the course in just under a minute. That equates to a 40-story drop with pressure in the turns of up to 5 Gs of force. Both places offer bobsled rides in the summer as well. They put the sleds on wheels and run them down the course at speeds up to 70 miles per hour. Either way, you're guaranteed a rush! Contact: Lake Placid Olympic Region, (518) 523-4436; or Utah Olympic Park, (435) 658-4200.

American Clippers and Cutters

The first sleds mass-produced in the United States were made by the Paris Manufacturing Company in South Paris, Maine. The venerable company, founded by Henry Morton, operated continuously from 1861 to 1989. It began by producing a line of sleds and toboggans for the Maine and Boston markets. Morton originally made elegant clippers and cutters with steel-clad hardwood runners, all hand-painted by his wife.

For sled designs, Morton took horse-drawn sleighs as his models, reducing them to a size that could be pulled uphill and raced downhill by a boy or girl. The Yankee Clipper sleds had runners upturned at the front, ending in a point, and were designed to be "belly-whoppers," ridden face-first. Cutter sleds were taller, with runners that curved gracefully over the front of the sled deck, and were designed to be ridden sitting down. Both kinds of sled were difficult to steer; to turn them, one had to bend the runners (easier on the Clipper than on the Cutter) or put a foot down on one side or the other.

This glorious sledding era was captured by a *Harper's Weekly* article in 1875, in which it was announced that,

> The City Fathers of Boston, remembering the time when they were boys, have earned the gratitude of the youth of that goodly town by giving them a sliding course on the Common. The course is watered every night, after the merriment of the day is over, so that it presents a smooth glassy surface of ice.... The army of sleds is prodigious. There are long sleds, short sleds, and double-runners, from the rudest to the most elegant style of construction, and boys of all ages, sizes and complexions take part in the exhilarating pastime.... The excitement has spread through the whole city, and thousands of people throng the Common. There is racing and chasing over the key course, and when some lively little fellow skillfully steered his craft, and sped by his companions on the way, followed closely by a fleet of double-runners manned by about the jolliest set of grown men that ever straddled a sled, some shouting, others piping whistles and blowing horns, the young ladies, and even old men and women, caught by the inspiration, and their countenances plainly said, "I wish I were a boy!"

As time went on, the Paris Manufacturing Company expanded into making steerable runner sleds, along with double-runner bobsleds, baby sleighs, and skis. In fact, Paris Manufacturing was the first commercial maker of skis in the United States, supplying skis to the Army during World War I and World War II.

A victim of changing times, Paris Manufacturing went bankrupt in 1989, and a fire in 1990 destroyed the original plant. In 1991, Canadian-owned sled maker Torpedo set up its United States sales and distribution center at the site of the former Paris plant.

ROSEBUD, THE MOST FAMOUS SLED IN HOLLYWOOD

The 1941 film classic *Citizen Kane* revolves around a Yankee Clipper sled named Rosebud. At the end of the movie, the last thought of billionaire Charles Foster Kane is of a childhood gift from his mother, a sled that meant more to him than anything else in the world.

Rosebud was actually a prop made of light balsa wood. Three copies were made from a single hardwood prototype, two of which burned during the filming of the movie. The one remaining sled was bought by Steven Spielberg in 1986 for $60,500. Its hardwood prototype sold at auction in 1996 for $233,500.

The Legendary Flexible Flyer

It's a rare person who does not immediately recognize the name "Flexible Flyer" and associate it with winter, snow, and kids. In retrospect, it seems to have happened very quickly, but at the time it was hard to imagine the sled would become such a huge success.

As the story goes, in 1889, inventor and successful farm implement manufacturer Samuel Leeds Allen submitted a patent for a sled with a slatted seat and a pair of metal runners, weakened at one point about halfway back to form a sort of hinge. The smallest Flexible Flyer sled retailed for $2.50, while the largest had foot rests for three adults and sold for $6.00. Allen advertised his new Flexible Flyer far and wide, but toy buyers for large department stores said the new sled was "not practical." Within Allen's farm equipment business, resistance to the sled was strong as well. His salesmen complained that selling sleds cut their vacations short. In actuality, they found toy buyers a much tougher class to handle than buyers of farm equipment. They encouraged Allen to sell the patent but he refused.

Given this resistance, Allen stopped marketing the sled for several years. In the early 1900s a revival of interest in golf, tennis, skating, tobogganing and other outdoor sports led Allen to think the time was finally ripe for his sled, too. He began to market the Flexible Flyer sled again, and in almost no time, hit the jackpot by landing accounts at two big department stores, Wanamaker's in Philadelphia and Macy's in New York City. Sales of the Flexible Flyer grew exponentially, soaring above everyone's predictions. Just before Christmas of 1915, Allen described the company's sales in a letter to his wife: "We have been selling sleds at a great pace, averaging right along about 2,000 per day, and the demand so urgent we are sending whole car loads of about 1,200 each to New York, New Haven, and Pittsburgh by express: perhaps five full cars in all. There seems to be little doubt but that we will sell out clean, in all about 120,000; and it also seems likely that the dealers will also sell out clean." In that year, retail prices for the sleds ran as high as $12.00 for the No. 6, an eight-and -a-half foot long, forty-one pound sled designed to carry six adults.

As sleds became a must-have holiday gift and the United States entered a period of unprecedented prosperity, sales kept climbing and a dozen other competitors quickly entered the market, including Standard Novelty Works' "Lightning Guider" sled and Paris Manufacturing's "Speedaway" sled, both steerable metal-runner sleds.

Allen worked to stay ahead of his competitors by forming partnerships with prominent figures and creating new sled models. In 1927, the year Charles Lindbergh made the first solo, non-stop flight from New York to Paris, the company introduced a Plucky Lindy model with the slogan, "Out front among Lindbergh's."

In 1928, six Flexible Flyers made it to the South Pole with famed polar explorer Admiral Richard E. Byrd. In 1935, Allen came out with Splitkein wooden skis and the Flexy Racer, a sled on wheels, designed to be used in the summertime. In 1938, Donald Duck and Mickey Mouse-branded sleds were created. In 1940, Allen produced his final innovation, the Ski Racer, a sled with a pair of long, flexible skis beneath a classic Flexible Flyer seat. Riders would lie down on the seat and steer by holding the tips of the skis in their hands.

Samuel Allen's family sold the sled business in 1968, and it passed through the hands of several owners over the next 30 years. Flexible Flyer sleds are still made today, although they now compete in a retail world filled with lower-cost plastic sleds.

AN ALL-AMERICAN SLED TOWN

My hometown of Silverton has just one paved main street, and often that street is snow-packed from snowstorms whirling over the Colorado Rockies. The rest of town has roads that are nicely graded gravel in the short summer, and hard-packed snow all winter long. Without doubt, the best way to get around town is on a kicksled—especially if you are sitting on the sled while someone else kicks! People young and old like kicksleds because they require almost no balance and let you move with stability across incredibly slippery surfaces. We even have a group in town of older women in their 60's and 70's who go out kicksledding together in the evenings when the streets ice up.

One of the favorite events of our long winter is the Kicksled Rodeo, which takes place on an almost-always sunny Saturday morning in February. Over one hundred people (that's a lot for a town of 450 residents), many in full costume, compete in a range of serious and hilarious contests. There are sprints and endurance races, relay races with a rider and a kicker (they switch halfway through), races with kids, and races among kids. These are followed by the raucous dog race, with dogs held on leashes while their owners hold on tight to both dog and kicksled. Invariably the event ends in a tangle of barking dogs, fallen sleds, and laughing sledders. For the finale, teams compete in kicksled acrobatics, a form of kicksled ballet with several people trying to coordinate graceful moves while sliding along on a single kicksled.

One of Silverton's other fine features is a small, town-owned ski area. It's so close to town that it's no more than 15 blocks from anyone's house. While you can't sled on the ski runs (during the day, anyway), there are demarcated sledding runs on the slopes. One of them is steep enough to be able to catch air under your sled off the bump in the middle—and earn the applause of people watching from the deck of the lodge! Late at night, in a practice barely tolerated by local officials, dedicated sledding groups head to the ski area for moonlight sledding. Each run ends with the grande finale of sliding at top speed through the empty parking lot and out toward the Animas River.

Let's Go
Sledding!

*A*s a sledmaker, I know which sleds I like, but if in doubt, take what you've got in the garage and go sledding! Actually, I've probably gone sledding on almost every imaginable object, from cafeteria trays to blocks of ice (perfect on a golf course in summer). Yet there's no question that different sled types offer different experiences. You can divide sleds into two groups, those that are steerable and those that aren't.

Steerable Sleds

My personal favorites among these highly maneuverable sleds, such the Mountain Boy Ultimate Flyer, are made with plastic or metal runners. They're essentially skis or skids that allow the rider to steer at will, swooping down hills in wide curves.

The Flexible Flyer is still a classic sled, with moderate steerability. Because it has thin metal runners, it works only on hard-packed snow or ice. In fresh or lightly packed snow, the runners just sink and you can't go anywhere. One of the best aspects of this sled, however, is the sound its metal runners make clacking along on the ice, a symphonic accompaniment to your acceleration.

A Hammerhead sled is comfortable and light, and turns quickly. It has four skis beneath its bed, with the front two skis connected by a handlebar. The handlebar is in turn linked to the rear part of the sled by a flexible coupling that provides spring-loaded steering. Built of aluminum tubing and high-tech plastics, the sled has a sleek, modern design.

The inflatable Airboard is a great sled for jumping, since its air-filled bed ensures soft landings. It operates on the same principle as a black rubber inner tube, but its wedge shape and grooved rubber base make it more steerable, while its base material is much more durable.

The Mountain Boy Ultimate Flyer has a slippery plastic bottom and full-pivot steering, while the Classic Flyer takes the Flexible Flyer's design a step further, using metal runners and adding a second pivot point to make it even more steerable.

I keep looking for a steerable all-plastic sit-upon sled that is designed so that adults can use it with their kids. But what I've found are mostly one-kid sleds with steering wheels, and a front ski that does the turning—my favorite looks like a Ferrari. For the best quality all-plastic sleds, look for the Eurosled brand.

Non-Steerable Sleds

Surprisingly, however, most sleds on the market can't be steered, or at least not steered well. Regardless of sled type, you can almost always use your hands to slow down one side of the sled or the other, turning it a few degrees left or right. On a disc or inner tube, this can lead to dizzying results if you start spinning, and I've known more than a few who do this on purpose.

Many companies make toboggans. These are typically beautiful wooden sleds, flat-bottomed and smooth riding, perfect for a big family outing. They are nearly impossible to steer, but they can handle many different kinds of snow and terrain. Be sure to add a pad for comfort.

Davos are elegant, classic Swiss sleds that have much in common with the Olympic luge. You sit on them and steer with the inside of your lower leg, bending the front of the sled itself to make a gradual turn.

Discs come in both metal and plastic, and can be a lot of fun on slight slopes. On steeper slopes, it's very difficult to stay on the disc, and steering of any kind is impossible.

There are one hundred plus varieties of injection-molded plastic sleds designed primarily to be inexpensive and get kids down the sledding hill. These plastic tubs, as I like to refer to them, are widely available at your hardware or grocery store. Confession: I bought the bright purple one.

Inner tubes are easy, fun, and fast, but really not recommended. Sledding can be a dangerous sport, and I have found inner tubes are the most dangerous of all sled options. Landing after taking a jump in one is particularly violent, as your back almost always bends the wrong way over the inner tube.

TO SLED OR NOT TO SLED?

In doubt about whether you can go sledding? Here are a few ordinary items you can find around the house that will let you slide down the hill and have fun even without an authentic sled.

- Plastic cafeteria trays: Plain, ubiquitous, and slippery as can be. Most kids can fit themselves onto one, while adults do better sitting on one and putting their feet on another. Lying down across three or four trays works too, but it's best if you put down a towel first for padding.

- Garbage can lids: Plastic ones are much better than metal. They'll slide like snow discs, but are often bigger and don't spin as much.

- Canoes: Seriously. A friend of mine once surprised a big gathering by sliding down a steep snow-packed slope in a canoe. The only problem was, he couldn't stop and barreled right through the crowd.... No, no one was hurt.

- Other water toys, such as boogie boards and inflatable beach inner tubes: All are very slippery, hard to steer, and not very durable, but they work when nothing else is around.

- Snow or grain shovels: You will be impressed by how fast you can travel down a hill sitting on a plastic grain scoop: The official world record is 67 miles per hour on a store-bought shovel. For the rest of us, it's just a simple way to slide back down the mountain.

- The seat of your snow pants: Last but not least. It's not for the faint of heart, but snow pants slide incredibly well, and as you bounce into the air you're guaranteed to find yourself laughing halfway down.

A Serious Sledder's Tips for Finding the Very Best Hill and the Best Snow

Unfortunately, the days are gone when you could sled almost anywhere. It now takes a little work to find a good sledding hill.

Snow conditions are very important, of course. A little bit of fresh snow (anything from a skiff to an inch) over a hard-packed surface offers the best sledding conditions. It's fast, quiet, and you feel like you're the first person to discover the joy of sledding. A warm spring day can also be wonderful with softer snow, bright sun, and slippery conditions.

If it hasn't snowed for a while, sledding hills can get very bumpy from intensive use, particularly if sledders walk right back up the course. It's not something that would keep me from sledding, of course, but I would look for the smoothest part of the hill.

And if my favorite sledding hill wasn't in good condition? I'd try a spot with a different aspect—that is, facing a different direction. Sunshine on south-

facing slopes makes them soft in the daytime and icy at night, but it can also melt the snow away. North-facing slopes hold snow the longest, but the snow there will also be less likely to pack down into a good sled run. If neither south nor north looks good? Try east- or west-facing slopes. Wind changes snow conditions as well. In my area of Colorado, the wind normally comes out of the southwest, so south- and west-facing slopes are often scoured down to dirt. Meanwhile, all that snow is blown onto the north- and east-facing slopes.

I evaluate a sledding hill based on a few key factors. First, how steep is it? For myself, I might want a very steep hill to ensure some downhill thrills, but the rest of the family might want something a little less extreme. Second, what does the snow look like? Is it smooth and fast, or hard and bumpy? Finally, I look for potential obstacles. Every good sledding hill is wide open, without trees, rocks or anything else to get in the way of a sensational run. The best hills also have a runout at the bottom, so sleds can decelerate on their own. Remember too, that if the sledding hill is crowded, you'll have to steer around all the other sledders and spectators.

Some possibilities for good sledding include:

- Golf courses or public parks: These areas typically feature smooth, rolling hills and often have the best runs when that first snow falls. It generally takes just a few inches of snow or even a thick frost, and you can have a safe but slippery slope.

- Ski areas: Most ski areas don't allow sledding of any kind. That said, often there are zones at the edge of the ski hills or adjoining the parking lot that are not actual ski runs, but are packed and sloped where you can get away with sledding. (Late at night, you may be able to sled on the ski runs themselves, but go forewarned: If you are caught, you may have to talk quickly to stay out of trouble.)

- Long driveways or seldom-used roads: Don't sled on a main thoroughfare! But other roads that are driven just once or twice a day may be relatively safe. Make sure you know enough about the road and its neighborhood to avoid any collisions, and don't sled around blind corners. Also, beware of trespassing. If in doubt, invite the property owner to come sledding with you.

- Public sledding hills: Public hills are a great community asset, but they can also be the bumpiest places to go sledding because they get so much use. With a little advance planning (sled pads!), however, these hills can be a lot of fun.

For the craziest of crazies, there's the He'e Holua, an ancient Hawaiian tradition of lava sledding. Traditionally, Hawaiians honored Pele, the goddess of fire, by climbing to the top of mile-long rock slopes. They would lie down or kneel on hardwood sleds measuring 12 inches wide and as much as 18 feet long, then descend downhill at incredible speeds. "You can't even imagine what it's like to be headfirst, 4 inches off the ground, doing 30, 40, 50 miles an hour on rock," says Tom "Pohaku" Stone, who is working to revive the ritual sport. "It looks like you are riding on fluid lava. It's death-defying ... but it's a lot of fun."

NO·SNOW SLEDDING

Why let the lack of snow keep you from sledding? It can be truly delightful to rocket down a slope in the middle of summer. Consider the following warm-weather options.

- Ice blocks on a grassy slope: Buy a block at your local convenience store, fold up a towel, and put it on top of the block. Then sit on the towel and splay out your feet and hands. Watch out! Ice blocks slide incredibly fast.

- Cardboard boxes on grass: This works best on a hot, dry day because that's when the cardboard and grass are most slippery. Be very careful that your course has no rocks in it, and don't count on being able to steer.

Sledding Style

Sledding Style and Comfort

To get the most out of sledding, it's essential not be stuck with one sledding approach or position. Try heading downhill several different ways to see what works best and feels most comfortable to you.

Lying Down: Face First

For the fastest, most exhilarating ride, lie down on the sled face-first. With minimal wind resistance and your face inches above the snow, it doesn't matter what speed you are going—it will feel fast! If you are on a steerable sled, this position also gives you the most leverage on the steering handle. Always wear gloves, and keep your hands loose on the handle so you can move them if an ice clump or rock is likely to hit your fingers. If the snow is light and powdery, push up on your elbows to lift your head and keep the snow out of your face. My favorite thing to do—riding this way with a small child on my back. I get the fun of fast sledding, and they get to be up high, out of any blowing snow.

Lying Down: Feet First

This actually works much better than you might think, and you can imagine yourself on the luge course. Lie down on your back, with your feet pointing downhill. Don't put your feet on the steering handles; you will steer by pulling on the rope. Hold the rope in your hands, lift your head up enough to look down the hill, and pull on the rope as needed to turn the sled. The last time I went sledding this way, I forgot to tuck in my pants and jacket. Because both were held open by the wind as I went downhill, they filled with snow. Brrr!

The Seated Position

Start out by sitting upright on the sled, with your legs stretched out in front of you (or crossed under you if on a disk). If there's a steering bar, brace your feet on it so they have good leverage. If you're putting several people on the sled, the person in front should sit cross-legged or put their feet out over the front of the sled, while the next or second person on the sled uses their feet to steer. If I'm on a runner sled with a young child, I put her right in front of me.

Multiple Riders

On a longer sled such as a toboggan, you can often fit three or four adults. Wrap your feet around the person in front of you, and hold on! If the toboggan has ropes running along the sides, grab these. Remember the person in the front has to yell which way for everyone to lean when you go around curves. On smaller sleds, it's also possible (and good fun) to stack several people lying down. For instance, I know a couple who sleds together on an Ultimate Flyer. He lies belly-down first, then she lies down on top of him. You wouldn't believe how fast they go.

Basic Steering Techniques

To turn a steerable sled, it's easy—just turn the steering bar. With any other sled, you can steer it somewhat by using a combination of braking and leaning. By putting your hands out onto the snow on the right side, you will turn right and vice versa. For more turning power, lean right to turn right. To steer a disc or inner tube, don't let yourself go backwards! Put both hands down on the snow, and just push harder with one hand instead of the other to steer in the desired direction.

To stop, use your feet and hands. If necessary, roll off the sled before it runs into something. Of course, one of the great joys of sledding is to yell loudly whether you're about to hit something or not!

DRESSED TO SLED

In the 1800s and 1900s, people dressed up to go sledding, or coasting, as the pastime was commonly called back then. Photographs from the period show winter revelers dressed as smartly as if they were attending church. Ladies wore feminine dresses with full skirts, bustles, tight waists and high collars typical of the Victorian and Edwardian eras' fashionable hourglass silhouette. Topped with capes and short jackets, bonnets, high buttoned boots, and gloves completed a proper sledding outfit. Men wore dashing tailored suits with capes and overcoats. Top hats were not uncommon on sledding hills either. Clearly, sledding in this time was a social event as much as a sport. We're not so fashion-conscious today, but it still makes sense to dress well for playing in the snow:

- Fleece or wool hat to keep your ears toasty.
- Gloves or mittens with a waterproof exterior, but not so thick you can't steer.
- Turtleneck tops or a cozy neck-up to keep your neck warm. (Scarves aren't recommended since they can fly off or get caught in sled runners.)
- Thick water-resistant outer jacket. (Choose one without a hood that could get caught on sled runners.)
- Water-resistant snow pants! A sledder's best friend. They'll keep you warmer and drier than long underwear and jeans.
- Warm, waterproof boots. These should tie or secure in other ways so they don't slip off if you use a foot to steer or stop.

And don't forget helmets! It seems everyone I talk to about sledding has some scar from a childhood sled outing. Wearing a helmet makes sledding much safer. Your biking or skiing helmet will work just fine.

The Virtues and Benefits of Sledding Etiquette

Get out of the way! You might have the newest, most steerable sled on the market, but unfortunately, it won't keep the kid on an inner tube from running into you. Sledding hills are managed chaos. Well, maybe just chaos.

There are two basic rules in sledding, which you could reasonably call rules of survival as well as etiquette. First, watch out for sledders coming towards you and your children, and stay off to the side as much as possible when climbing back up the hill. Second, you absolutely must avoid all other people when you are sledding downhill, even if it means rolling off your sled and sending it into the woods.

To be well-loved at your sledding hill, do a bit more. Help other people get up when they crash, bring an extra thermos of hot chocolate, and pull the neighborhood kids back up the hill. Your winter will be sweet.

Advanced Techniques

One of the great pleasures of sledding is that you don't have to be good to have a great time. Just get on your sled and head downhill. But, if you're inclined to do some more extreme sledding, a little technique will help. Here's how to make a sharp turn on a steerable sled such as an Ultimate Flyer or Flexible Flyer, which makes everything else possible. With a little practice, you'll have a repertoire of sledding techniques in no time.

SHARP TURNS

STEP 1. A key part of steering is pushing the back part of the sled left and right with your legs. Before you start your run, lie down on the sled and splay your legs out over the sled deck. The insides of your legs should just touch the back corners of the sled. Make sure you're comfortable.

STEP 2. I like to start by heading the sled crosswise to the slope. Then when I want to head straight down, I just turn the sled downhill. Start your turn with the front of the sled, turning it left for this example. Once the turn has begun, shift your weight to the uphill or left-hand side of the sled, and push the back of the sled into the turn with your left leg.

SLALOMING

Once you've made a good turn to the left, change direction by turning the front of the sled to the right. Then shift your weight uphill and push with your right leg against the back of the sled.

TRAVERSING

With practice, you can guide the sled at an angle across a steep slope without falling off. If you are going right across the slope, keep your weight on the uphill or right-hand side of the sled. Use your right leg to push against the back of the sled and to keep youself from sliding off.

HOCKEY STOP

Once you feel the sled turning strongly, push even harder with your leg against the back of the sled. If the conditions are right, you'll find that the back of the sled skids into the turn until you are perpendicular to the hill and stopped. Nice work!

BUILDING JUMPS

For sledding jumps, you want a low-angle jump with a steep downhill landing. In other words, you don't want to take the sled too high into the air, because landing hurts. With a properly built jump, you can spend considerable time in the air and be only a foot or so above the snow. Don't worry that it won't be enough fun! Taking a jump at high speeds is always exciting.

KITE SLEDDING

With kite-surfing growing in popularity, I had to try kite sledding. If you are experienced with kites, adding a sled is simple. Get your kite into the air, sit down on the sled with your feet on the handlebar, and start sledding. For this technique, you'll want a wide-open, windy area, preferably a frozen lake. While this method is basically simple, it ultimately wasn't for me. I catapulted face-first off the sled and onto the ice.

POWDER SLEDDING

Sleds with broad, flat bottoms do very well in powder. The question is, how you will get back up the hill? If you've got a packed trail or road to get back to the top, you'll enjoy some terrific powder sledding. Pick a good steep hill, and sit on your sled, but don't lie down. Put your weight on the back of the sled, and start heading downhill. Drag your hands in the snow as necessary, and put your feet on the handlebar, if there is one, to steer.

Red Flags and Warnings! Watch Out for Sledding Dangers

One night some high-school friends and I were sledding at an abandoned ski area near Vail, Colorado. We had only inner tubes, big, black and blown up tight. It was a well-known sledding area, but there were several feet of fresh snow over the slopes and only a few tracks. After a long hike up the central packed sled run, we clambered onto our tubes and readied ourselves for the ride. Three of us decided to link together, one person's feet holding onto the next person's inner tube.

We knew inner tubes couldn't be steered, but on this, our first run of the night, we didn't consider the implications. We quickly found out that sleds, including trains of inner tubes, move much faster when they are long and heavy. And, if for some reason you leave the track and head into powder, you create a cloud of snow making it impossible to see or even to breathe.

Heading down the main track, we picked up speed —fearsome speed, enough that we almost jumped off our tubes. But for whatever crazy reason, we stayed and held on. Although we tried to steer, we quickly left the track and slid into deep powder, heading like greased lightning straight downhill toward a clump of trees. I was on the last tube and caught one final glimpse of the trees dead ahead before we were engulfed in a blizzard of snow, not slowing down at all. Luckily, with a quick shout to each other, we rolled off our inner tubes just in time, and they skidded on into the trees without us. It was my first lesson about how sledding can be dangerous.

Even on a steerable sled, there may be dangers on the slope you'll need and want to avoid. Trees, unfortunately, don't move when you hit them. It's imperative to avoid them in every way possible. Ditto for roots, rocks and signs. If there are others sledding on your hill, be constantly aware of where the people, their dogs, and their sleds are going. (Remember that sleds occasionally rocket down hills without their owners.)

As far as other unanticipated dangers, since many of the places you might be sledding are private property, it's worth keeping a lookout for the golf-course caretaker. If he arrives, you can at least streak by him on your last run.

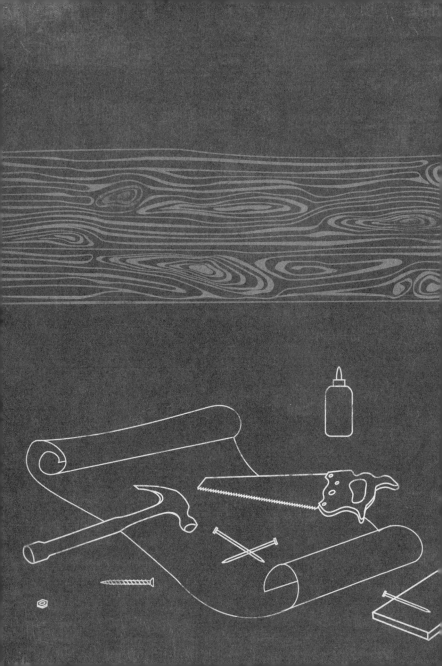

Building a Better Sled

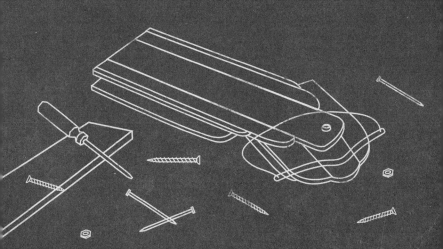

I grew up in Grand Junction, Colorado. My parents were (and are) avid skiers, so we spent every weekend at the local ski area. I love to ski, but confess I often quit early to go sledding. My sled as a kid was an old Flexible Flyer sled, much-repaired but still workable. If I was lucky, the sledding conditions were perfect—an open slope of hard-packed, icy snow. The sled would roar down the hill. If you pointed it in the right direction and pulled as hard as you could on the steering bar, you could almost get it to turn when you had to—almost. But much of the time we had new, soft snow, and the slope under the fresh snow wasn't hard-packed. The sled's metal runners would sink right in, and it would go slowly or not move at all. When I got older, I switched to a plastic sled—just a long tub, but it worked like a champ on soft snow. Ah, if only it would turn! Back then, I laid out a number of designs for sleds that would float through soft snow, race down hard-packed slopes, and turn easily. I pictured an articulated toboggan. I drew a sled with raised outriggers. You turned that one by tipping it to the side and engaging one of the outriggers. I didn't get a chance to build any of them, however—not for another 30 years.

My parents long ago despaired of me following a straight and narrow path. I majored in Mandarin Chinese at college, went on to become an environmental consultant in charge of biological studies for the Hualapai Tribe in the Grand Canyon, and ran my own business writing and publishing newsletters.

When I got the chance to move to Silverton, high in the Rocky Mountains of southwestern Colorado, I jumped at it—moved as fast as I could, sold the newsletter business, and set up shop to begin making sleds.

In the Beginning: Kicksleds

I started with kicksleds because I already had a template and a market. People all around town were already using kicksleds imported from Sweden, but the local supplier had recently closed shop. Kicksleds look strange at first, like a chair on runners. Until you've kicked one and sped off over snowy roads, it's hard to imagine how easy and fun they are to use. I rented some unheated shop space from a friend, took careful measurements of a Swedish kicksled, and started production.

As you might guess, it took a while to actually begin producing kicksleds. I had some woodworking skills, but I knew nothing about bending and welding steel runners. After several days of heating and pounding steel bars, I befriended a local welder who took my twisted prototype kicksled runner and began turning out beautiful, flawless runners. What a pleasure to have help from someone who knew their craft!

My first kicksleds weren't perfect, but I couldn't produce them fast enough for everyone who wanted one. I kept making them one by one through January of that first winter, settling on Mountain Boy as a name and creating a signature look—natural willow handles, thick hardwood construction, hand-worked steel runners—and using a branding iron to burn in the Mountain Boy logo. I found a few retail stores in the area willing to carry my sleds. To expand the sales market, I put a kicksled on wheels so I could push it around the convention center floor at a big trade show in Salt Lake City. I hoped to develop a business based on a single type of sled—but I still had a long way to go!

Building the First Ultimate Flyer, the Hard Way

That February, as winter deepened and temperatures inside my shop dropped below zero, demand for kicksleds slowed and I finally had a chance to work on my idea for a highly steerable sled, one that would float through soft snow and fly across hardpack. I knew the best-steering sleds were bobsleds, which have a front set of runners that can turn back and forth like the front wheels of a car. And the best sleds in variable snow conditions were still those simple plastic tubs. Their wide surface floats on soft snow, and their bottom ridges enable them to zip even faster on hard snow or ice.

Viewed from the top, my new sled design was reminiscent of a classic Flexible Flyer. It had a curved handle with plenty of room for your hands or feet, a sturdy wooden deck that would support several people, and straight hand rails along the sides so passengers could hold on. From the bottom, however, this sled was totally different. It was really two sleds, one long and one short, joined at a single pivot point with a strong stainless-steel bolt. Each section was about five inches thick, with a curved front and scalloped back. The sides were wooden, but the bottom surface that touched the snow was covered with a thick layer of slippery plastic. To increase the turning power and give the sled purchase on ice, thin stainless steel blades projected below the edges of the sled.

As I tested the sled on the snowy hills around town, it met all my criteria. It was fast, and it turned so well you had to be gentle or the sled would flip sideways. Best of all, it floated through powder while it carved across ice. It was also a handsome sled, if I do say so myself.

In September of that year, I christened the new sled The Ultimate Flyer. I also had a better shop outfitted with a woodstove, and an enthusiastic crew making both kicksleds and the Ultimate. I took off on marketing trips across Colorado, and succeeded in getting the Ultimate into a number of high-end sporting goods stores. The challenge now was getting the sleds built for delivery. If I'd only known what I was up against, or that things would become even more difficult!

I had designed the Ultimate Flyer the only way I knew how, using a framework of wood with a veneer of adhesive-backed plastic on the bottom. Like a piece of furniture, it had many pieces, each one joined by screws. But unlike a piece of furniture, the sled's weight had to be kept to a minimum, and it had to withstand the elements. This combination required using thin hardwood pieces, each one sealed with three coats of polyurethane.

When I added everything up, each sled consisted of 110 pieces of wood, 8 pieces of steel, 2 pieces of plastic, and 87 screws. Every sled took 10 man-hours to build. While they were beautiful and performed well, they just weren't versatile or strong enough. In fact, I received a letter from a woman who had bought matching sleds for her two kids. She wrote that when they took them out sledding, they didn't work. The snow froze to the metal blades as if there were brakes mounted on the bottom of the sleds. At that point, I came close to throwing in the towel. Instead, I decided to rework my design.

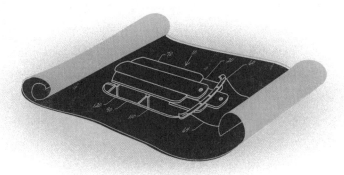

Success on the Second Try!

I remember clearly the comment from my plastics supplier, an old friend: "You could take the easy way out and just mold a piece of plastic for the bottom instead of having that complicated assembly," he said. Eureka! Because I hadn't known how to mold plastic, I hadn't even considered it as a possibility.

With a single plastic piece on the bottom—well, actually two pieces, one on the front section and one on the back—the sled would work better. Just as astonishing, I could cut the sled's price in half. Within two weeks, my plastics buddy showed me how to make a mold (out of wood, to my surprise) and I created one with a curved front, a wide flat area, and raised ridges on the sides to act as runners. He thermoformed a layer of plastic over the mold. I mounted it on a sled deck and checked snow conditions on my favorite hills.

That day, I intended to go sledding for a few short runs, simply to test the new prototype. But two hours later I was still out on the slopes. The new Ultimate Flyer worked so much better than I expected. I could slalom down the hill, and as I slowed down at the bottom, I could turn it completely around or make a flashy hockey stop. It didn't take me long to decide to go for a longer run. Towing the new sled, I headed three miles up a steep snow-packed road maintained by our local snowmobile club—and sledded all the way down without stopping! For the first time, I was convinced I had a winner. The Ultimate sold well the next winter, and Mountain Boy's future once again looked bright.

Once I was reasonably sure the Ultimate would succeed, I wanted to re-work the Flexible Flyer design so it too was more steerable. In its heyday, the Flexible Flyer was remarkable because it steered at all. But even at its best the sled could only execute a 10-degree turn. That's enough to follow a curvy road, but not enough to slalom down a hill or have confidence you'll avoid obstacles in your path. Also, as toys in general became cheaper, the reliable sturdiness of the Flexible Flyer went downhill as its manufacturer tried to keep the retail price low. Still, I figured there was a market for a well-made, fast-turning runner sled. At the very least, I'd get to test it out!

As I laid the frame of the Ultimate Flyer over metal runners, I realized I might be able to use its design to add steering leverage. The traditional Flexible Flyer has one pivot point, at the very tip of the sled. I kept this one, and added another further down the sled's deck. Dual pivot points would give the rider more than twice as much power to turn the runners.

When I tested the first prototype, I found that I could bend the runners into a full arc with little effort. On my first run, I took sharp corners at top speed, slalomed down the hill, and even turned circles. With practice, I could do a hockey stop on ice, bringing the sled to a halt within seconds. Instead of feeling like a scary, uncontrollable sled, riding the new and improved Flexible Flyer felt like wearing a pair of just-sharpened ice skates.

Since that time I've designed and built another half-dozen kinds of sleds. One of the things I've enjoyed most about making sleds—sturdy sleds, designed to last—is that they are things of value. The wood is not only strong, but it gains character with every scrape and dent. Sledding stories accumulate as the sled and the children grow older. From a practical point of view, if any piece of the sled breaks or wears out, it can be easily replaced. Even if the sled spends a decade or two in the garage, the next generation can pull it out and have the time of their lives.

At the Mountain Boy workshop, we make sleds from August through March. We work in a small shop, much smaller than you might imagine. If there are three of us in there, it's mighty tight. Many winter mornings we have to clear a path through several feet of snow just to reach the door of the shop. As Christmas approaches, the days get shorter, meaning we often arrive at the shop in darkness and leave long after the sun has set behind the mountains. But a few things help make the shop one of my favorite places:

- Satellite radio plays every kind of music under the sun.

- A crackling wood stove keeps the shop toasty warm, burns all the scraps we can't use, and also keeps the branding iron hot. (Each sled is literally branded by hand with the Mountain Boy logo.)

- The air is filled with the fragrances of different woods, from ash and maple to Spanish cedar and African padauk.

- With many repetitive tasks, there's plenty of time for lively conversation and for watching through the big glass windows as the snowstorms roll in.

Old-World Craftsmanship Overseas

Nowadays, we make high-end, specialty sleds in the Silverton workshop, while Mountain Boy sleds are also made in Huangyan, China, by my good friend Yu Guanglin and his crew. In his small, family-run workshop, he makes sleds the same way we do—by hand, paying attention to the beauty of the wood, selecting the best materials, getting all the details right. He buys sustainably harvested birch logs, and has planks cut from them to just the right thickness. The sawdust is used to fire the wood-drying kiln, so there's very little waste. In his shop, he carefully prepares all the materials: each plank is planed by hand, and each willow branch is peeled and sanded by his crew. When he assembles the sleds, he makes sure that all the parts match and have no flaws.

Après-Sled

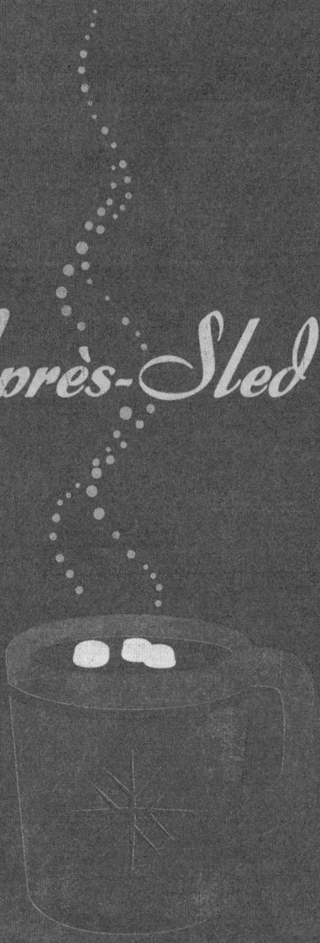

After a full day of sledding, you won't wonder whether it's good exercise. You'll be exhausted! To hold onto the glow from the day, I recommend a warm fire, hot cocoa or toddies, and an evening of telling tall tales with friends—about sledding, of course!

The Best Hot Cocoa

It doesn't get much better than the old-fashioned classic that's everyone's childhood favorite.

Makes 6 — 8 ounce servings

1/4 cup unsweetened, Dutch process cocoa powder
1/2 cup sugar
pinch of salt
1/3 cup hot water
4 cups whole milk
3/4 teaspoon vanilla extract
whipped cream for topping, if desired

In a medium saucepan, stir together cocoa, sugar and salt; slowly stir in hot water to blend ingredients. Bring to a boil over medium heat, stirring constantly. Boil and stir for 2 minutes. Add milk, while continuing to heat and stir. Be careful not to boil once milk has been added. Remove from heat and add vanilla. Beat with a rotary beater until foamy. Serve hot topped with a dollop of whipped cream.

The Sledmaker's
Hot Toddy Recipe

This drink is guaranteed to induce a warm after-sledding glow.

Makes 4 quarts

1 quart Ben & Jerry's vanilla ice cream, softened
1 pound organic butter
1 pound brown sugar
1 pound powdered sugar
2 teaspoons freshly ground nutmeg
2 teaspoons ground cinnamon
Meyer's Dark Rum
Boiling water

In a large bowl, mix together all ingredients except the rum and water.

For 1 serving, in an 8-ounce mug, gently stir together 1 ounce of rum and 4 tablespoons of the frozen mix; fill the mug with boiling water and stir again.

Freeze any of the unused ice cream mixture to make more hot toddies after the next time you go sledding. It will keep frozen for up to four months.

(adapted from the Colorado Cache Cookbook *by the Junior League of Denver)*

Sledding Movies

CITIZEN KANE: The 1941 classic with Orson Welles, centered on the sled "Rosebud." Highly recommended.

MONSTERS, INC.: An animated children's movie with a fabulous sledding scene in the middle.

COOL RUNNINGS: Inspired by the true story of Jamaica's Olympic bobsledding team with some outstanding sledding scenes.

SNOW DOGS: Features Cuba Gooding Jr. and some good dog-sledding scenes.

IRON WILL: An inspirational story for all ages about a young boy trying to win a dog sled race.

Sledding Books

WINTERDANCE: The Fine Madness of Running the Iditarod, by Gary Paulsen. There are dozens of books about dog sledding, but this is my favorite. It's the hilarious story of a Minnesota trapper who somehow gets the crazy idea he should try to run Alaska's famed Iditarod dog sled race.

SLEDDING ON BOSTON COMMON: A Story From the American Revolution, by Louise Borden. A children's book based on local folklore with beautiful watercolor illustrations by Robert Andrew Parker.

SNIPP, SNAPP, SNURR AND THE YELLOW SLED, by Maj Lindman. Swedish author Lindman wrote and illustrated a series of picture books for children, featuring identical triplets and set in 1940s Sweden. In this simple, elegant story, the brothers work together to buy a sled they see in a shop window.

COLD-WEATHER COOKING, by Sarah Leah Chase. These hearty dishes will surely warm you up after long days of downhill skidding!

THE SNOWFLAKE: Winter's Secret Beauty, by Kenneth Libbrecht and Patricia Rasmussen. A key element to successful sledding! This fascinating book looks at the physics of snow and its early researchers, and reveals in photographs the design and structure of individual snowflakes.

My
Sledding Memories

_____

_____

_____

_____

_____

_____

_____

_____

_____

_____

_____

_____

_____

About the Author

Brice Hoskin was born and raised in Colorado, where he discovered his love of sledding, skiing and adventuring at an early age. In 2002, Brice founded Mountain Boy Sledworks, a business firmly rooted in his deep personal love for snow. His path to becoming a sledmaker was far from direct: after majoring in Mandarin Chinese, he left college to become a wildlife biologist and then a business writer. Today, he lives with his wife and two sons in Silverton, Colorado, where seeking out the nation's best sledding terrain has become a way of life.